Hi, I'm Anna. I live with Linda and Pete, my foster parents.
It's our school leavers' party next week.
I'm going to wear my purple skirt but I want a new top to go with it.
I've asked Linda to come with me to buy one.

"I'd love to go shopping with you," said Linda.

"But *you'll* have to choose, and I'm afraid you must pay for it out of your own money."

I thought hard. I had £20 saved up.

"OK," I said.

"So where shall we go?" asked Linda.

"We could try Bella. It has gorgeous clothes, but it's a bit expensive," I said.

"What about Clothes Junction and The Room? They're a lot cheaper," said Linda.

SHOPS
BELLA
THE ROOM ✓
CLOTHES JUNCTION ✓

So on Saturday we went into town.

I took my purple skirt with me.

We looked in Clothes Junction first. I saw two tops that I liked.

They were both size 10. That's my size.

I looked at the prices.

They were £19.99.

CLOTHES JUNCTION
£19.99
£19.99

"Try them on," said Linda. "See if they fit."

I tried on the green one first.

I showed Linda.

"How do the sleeves feel?" she asked.

The sleeves felt a bit tight and it didn't look good with my skirt.

The label said 'dry clean only'.

That was no use.

Then I tried on the white top.
It felt nice and the label said you could wash it.
"What do you think?" I asked.
"It's *OK*," said Linda. "But do you want to spend *all* your money on it?"
I wasn't sure.

So we went to The Room. There was a sale on.

I found a lovely yellow top. You could get it in blue too.

They were only £11.99 each. I tried on the yellow top.

It was a good fit. It felt nice, too.

BARGAINS
The Room
Sale

"I love this one," I said. "Which colour do you like best?"

"You must choose," said Linda.

"I'll get the yellow one," I said.

"It's lovely," said Linda. "I'd quite like one myself!"

Linda told me to go and pay for it.

She wanted to look at the jumpers.

SALE
Bargains
SALE GOODS
BUY ONE
GET
ONE FREE
SALE
£11.99
£11.99

When I got to the till I had a nice surprise.
"It's Buy One, Get One Free," said
the assistant.
That gave me an idea.

I got the blue top for Linda, in her size. She was really pleased. We couldn't wait to show Pete!